I0814080

An Imprint of Pop!
popbooksonline.com

American Indians

THE APACHE

by N.C. Barnes

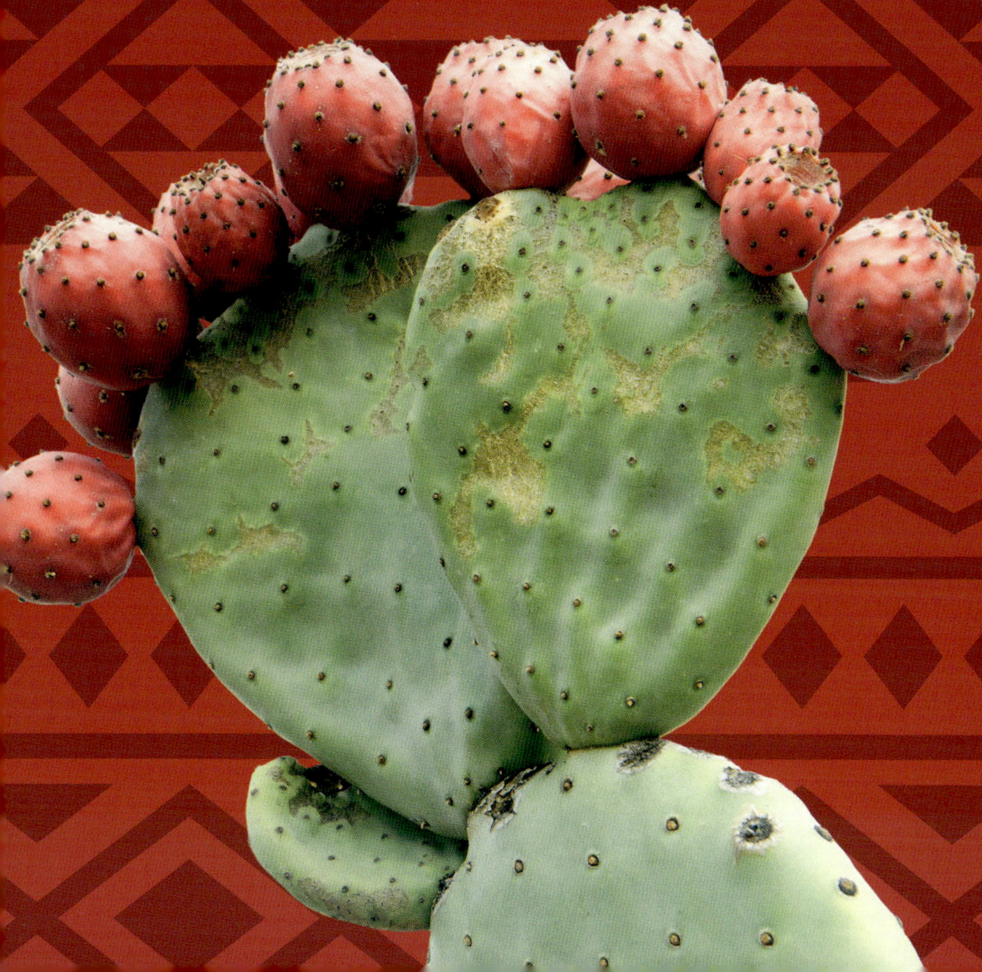

This book is filled with videos, puzzles, games, and more! Scan the QR codes* while you read, or visit the website below to make this book pop.

popbooksonline.com/Apache

abdobooks.com

Published by Pop!, a division of ABDO, PO Box 398166, Minneapolis, Minnesota 55439.

Printed in the United States of America, North Mankato, Minnesota.

052024
082024

THIS BOOK CONTAINS RECYCLED MATERIALS

Cover Photo: Getty Images
Interior Photos: Shutterstock Images, Getty Images, Alamy Stock Photo, Wikimedia
Editor: Emily Dreher
Series Designer: Colleen McLaren

Library of Congress Control Number: 2023947491

Publisher's Cataloging-in-Publication Data

Names: Barnes, N.C., author.
Title: The Apache / by N.C. Barnes
Description: Minneapolis, Minnesota : Pop!, 2025 | Series: American Indians | Includes online resources and index
Identifiers: ISBN 9781098246198 (lib. bdg.) | ISBN 9781098246754 (ebook)
Subjects: LCSH: Apache Indians--Juvenile literature. | American Indians--Juvenile literature. | Indians of North America--Juvenile literature. | Indigenous peoples--Social life and customs--Juvenile literature. | Cultural anthropology--Juvenile literature.
Classification: DDC 973.0497--dc23

*Scanning QR codes requires a web-enabled smart device with a QR code reader app and a camera.

TABLE OF CONTENTS

CHAPTER 1

WHO ARE THE APACHE?

Before European **settlers** came to North America, the land was wild and open. It was populated by American Indians. Each group had its own languages and **culture**.

Apache is the name used for certain groups of Athabaskan-speaking people.

WATCH A VIDEO HERE!

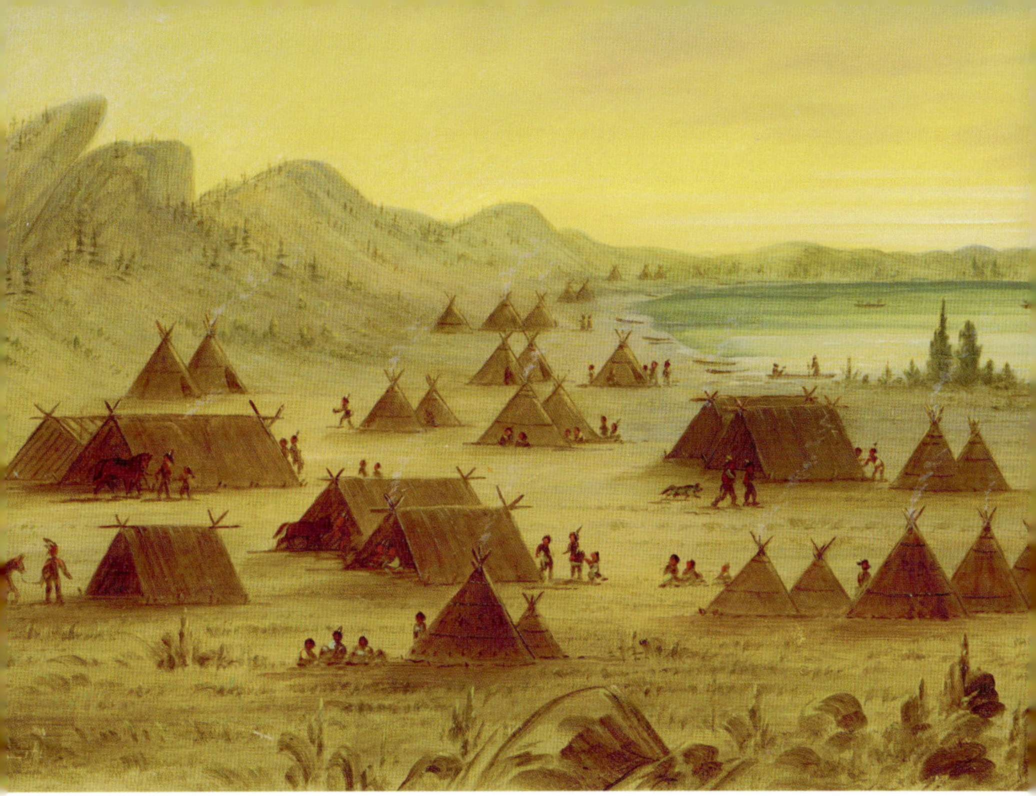

Languages are a common link between American Indian nations.

The Apache nation includes Mescalero, Jicarilla, Mimbreño, Chiricahua, Dilzhe'e (Tonto), Aravaipa, Coyotero, and Lipan American Indians.

DID YOU KNOW?

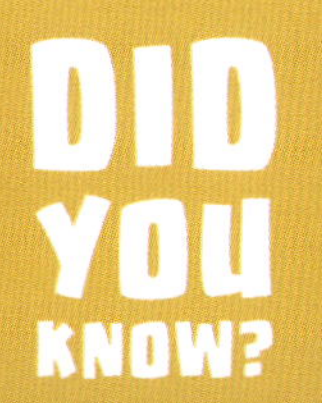

Jicarilla are referred to as Keepers of the Water.

Historical Apache land was mostly in the southwest United States and northern Mexico. Various bands lived in what is now New Mexico, Texas, Arizona, and Oklahoma. The Apache were originally from Canada. They moved south in 1200 CE.

It is known that Apache were from Canada because other people from there speak the same language

APACHE HOMELANDS

CANADA

UNITED STATES

HISTORICAL APACHE TERRITORY

The Apache lived in specific parts of the highlighted area.

ARIZONA

NEW MEXICO

OKLAHOMA

TEXAS

MEXICO

Family groups connected Apache people. Two to five families lived together in bands of ten to 50 people. Each band had a leader who reminded members of their duty to family and tradition. Bands would connect to each other through marriage. Connected bands formed tribes.

MARRIAGE

Getting married helped family groups build ties to each other. When a couple decided to marry, they went into the wilderness and lived together for two weeks. After that, they went to live with the woman's family. The man brought food for the whole family to share. Men and women from different family bands met each other at tribal **ceremonies** and celebrations.

Apache people refer to themselves as Nde. *It means "the people."*

CHAPTER 2

HISTORICAL LIFE

Apache people lived in wickiups. Wickiups were made with four long sticks stuck in the ground. They were bent and tied at the top to form a sturdy frame.

More sticks were placed around the frame and covered with plant fibers to create walls. There was a hole at the top of a wickiup to let smoke out.

LEARN MORE HERE!

Apache women were in charge of building homes.

DID YOU KNOW?

In colder winter months, animal hides covered the sides of wickiups to keep in warmth.

Wickiups were easy to set up and could be taken down quickly.

The Apache were nomadic. This means they moved from place to place. Bands of Apache people changed locations depending on what food was available at that time of year. They traveled on foot and eventually with the help of horses.

The portions of land where Apache lived received little rain. Despite this, Apache were experts at surviving on the few resources the desert gave them.

Bird feathers are held during important Apache ceremonies. The eagle feather is considered the most sacred.

Apache women were known for their ability to find water in even the driest of places.

Apache women were expert gatherers. They found acorns, seeds, cactus fruits, and plants. These gathered resources were used for food, building homes, and medicine. Men hunted foxes, deer, elk, turkeys, rabbits, and fish.

Apache people wore cotton clothes when weather was warm. Women wore wrap skirts and **ponchos**. Men wore **breechcloths**. When weather was cold, they wore deerskin clothes. Sometimes the Apache decorated their clothes with fringe and beads. Apache also made blankets and shawls.

Apache people were famous for their beautiful knee-high boots.

CHAPTER 3

FAMILY AND TRADITIONS

Children were deeply loved in Apache **culture**. Bands usually included only a few families. If a child was orphaned, they were immediately brought into another family.

Kachina dolls are given as gifts to young girls.

Apache children were taught good manners, kindness, and courage.

Cradleboards have been used by American Indians for thousands of years. They are still used today.

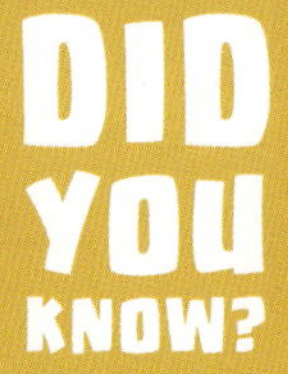

Some Apache children carried dolls in small versions of a cradleboard.

Babies were carried on their mother's back in a cradleboard. The mother's family usually made the cradleboards. They were decorated with beads.

Babies were wrapped tightly in the boards until they were old enough to walk. When families were working outside, they hung the cradleboard on a nearby tree.

Apache dolls were often made from cotton.

Once a child was old enough to walk, they helped their mother gather food, water, and wood. Girls learned to weave baskets, cook, and build wickiups. They worked with their mothers all their lives. Fathers and uncles taught boys to hunt, ride horses, and fight.

Woven baskets are lighter than pottery. They were easier to move around.

Baskets were originally made for family use. In the 1880s, Apache women began selling baskets to tourists.

Apache added beautiful art to everyday objects.

Apache bands are known for their basketmaking. Using desert shrubs, young trees, pine needles, cattails, and leaves, women wove baskets for all kinds of tasks. Some held food and belongings. Others were tightly woven and sealed with piñon tree sap to carry water.

Apache bands had some **spiritual** leaders. They led **ceremonies** honoring marriages, girls becoming women, and children's first steps.

Apache people honor four **sacred** mountains. They are the Sierra Blanca, Three Sisters Mountain, Oscura Mountain Peak, and Guadalupe Mountain.

The Apache wasted nothing they hunted and gathered. They made tools and beads from animal bones.

CHAPTER 4

WARRIORS FOREVER

The land the Apache lived on was **sparse**. They faced competition for goods by other American Indian bands. Sometimes their goods were stolen. Apache bands were known for leading raids on enemy groups. Apache warriors sneaked into enemy land and stole back what was taken from them.

COMPLETE AN ACTIVITY HERE!

Ceremonial dress worn today is called regalia.

Apache warriors traveled up to 70 miles (113km) a day.

Things became more difficult for Apache tribes when they first encountered European **settlers**. Europeans took over their hunting grounds. Apache were not able to get enough food to feed their families.

Raiding groups usually consisted of four to 12 men. They were experts at hiding, tracking enemies, and leaving no trace behind. They raided European settlements for food and other supplies that were taken from them.

In the 1800s, the United States took control of Apache land. The Apache were forced off their homeland. The US government made Apache families send their children away to schools. The schools treated them badly and tried to make them give up their **culture**. But Apache still fight to honor their traditions and way of life.

Battles between the Apache and the US lasted 40 years. They were called the Apache Wars.

The US forced the Apache nation onto **reservations**. Most Apache people now live in Arizona, New Mexico, and Oklahoma. Some Apache reservations have museums and culture centers that celebrate the people and land.

The Apache are proud of their history. Some still live their lives according to tradition.

MAKING CONNECTIONS

TEXT-TO-SELF

Apache children learned skills from their parents and family members. Have you learned any skills that way?

TEXT-TO-TEXT

Have you read about another American Indian nation? How is their culture similar to or different from the Apache people?

TEXT-TO-WORLD

The Apache people had to fight for their land when European settlers arrived. Can you think of any other cultural group who had to fight for the right to their own land?

GLOSSARY

breechcloth — a cloth worn over the groin.

ceremony — a formal event held on a special occasion.

culture — the customs, arts, and ideas of a group of people.

poncho — a blanket with a slit in the middle for the head so it can be worn as a sleeveless garment.

reservation — a piece of land set aside by the government for American Indians to live on.

sacred — something worthy of intense honor.

settler — a person who moves with a group of others to live in a new country or area. A place where settlers live is called a settlement.

sparse — not thickly grown.

spiritual — having to do with people's beliefs in things, such as the soul, nature, and what happens after death.

INDEX

DiscoverRoo!

ONLINE RESOURCES

This book is filled with videos, puzzles, games, and more! Scan the QR codes* while you read, or visit the website below to make this book pop.

popbooksonline.com/Apache

*Scanning QR codes requires a web-enabled smart device with a QR code reader app and a camera.